James H. Ruebush

Crowning Say

a varied collection of sacred songs for all occasions, especially for

evangelistic work, for the Sabbath-school, and the prayer-meeting

James H. Ruebush

Crowning Say

a varied collection of sacred songs for all occasions, especially for evangelistic work, for the Sabbath-school, and the prayer-meeting

ISBN/EAN: 9783337265670

Printed in Europe, USA, Canada, Australia, Japan

Cover: Foto ©Lupo / pixelio.de

More available books at **www.hansebooks.com**

THE
Crowning Day

A

VARIED COLLECTION OF SACRED
SONGS FOR ALL OCCASIONS

ESPECIALLY

FOR EVANGELISTIC WORK, FOR THE SABBATH-
SCHOOL, AND THE PRAYER-
MEETING

EDITED BY

J. H. RUEBUSH, J. H. HALL,
AND
ALDINE S. KIEFFER

Dedication.

TO THE EVANGELISTS WHO PROCLAIM THE COMING DAY; TO THE MYRIAD HOST OF SABBATH SCHOOL TEACHERS AND SCHOLARS; THIS GOSPEL SONG BOOK, "THE CROWNING DAY," IS MOST RESPECTFULLY DEDICATED BY THE AUTHORS.

Copyright, March 20, 1894, by THE RUEBUSH-KIEFFER CO.

THE CROWNING DAY.

"Henceforth there is laid up for me a crown of righteousness, which the LORD, the righteous judge, shall give me at THAT DAY; and not to me only, but unto all them also that love his appearing." Paul's second letter to Timothy. iv c: 8 verse.

No. 1.   Coronation.

"But we see Jesus, who was made a little lower than the angels for the suffering of death, *crowned with glory* and honour." HEBREWS ii: 9.

Edward Perronet.   O. Holden.

1. All hail the pow'r of Je-sus' name, Let an-gels prostrate fall, Bring forth the roy-al di-a-dem, And crown Him Lord of all; Bring forth the roy-al di-a-dem; And crown Him Lord of all.
2. Let ev-'ry kin-dred, ev-'ry tribe, On this ter-res-trial ball, To Him all maj-es-ty as-cribe, And crown Him Lord of all; To Him all maj-es-ty as-cribe, And crown Him Lord of all.
3. Oh, that with yon-der sa-cred throng We at His feet may fall, We'll join the ev-er-last-ing song, And crown Him Lord of all; We'll join the ev-er-last-ing song, And crown Him Lord of all.

No. 2. I am Washed in the Blood.

Rev. Elisha A. Hoffman.   J. H. Hall.

1. I have been to Jesus to be cleans'd with pow'r, In the blood, . . . the precious blood, And I linger at the fount this very hour, At the fount of Jesus' blood.
2. I will walk in meekness at my Saviour's side, O the blood, . . . the precious blood, I will trust each moment in the Crucified, O the blood, the precious blood.
3. I will keep unspotted from the world and sin, Thro' the blood, . . . the precious blood, In the fountain flowing for the soul unclean, In the fount of Jesus' blood.

CHORUS.

I am washed in the blood, In the heart-cleansing
Hallelujah,   Hallelujah,
I am washed, in the blood,

Copyright, 1893, by John McPherson. By per.

I am Washed in the Blood. Concluded.

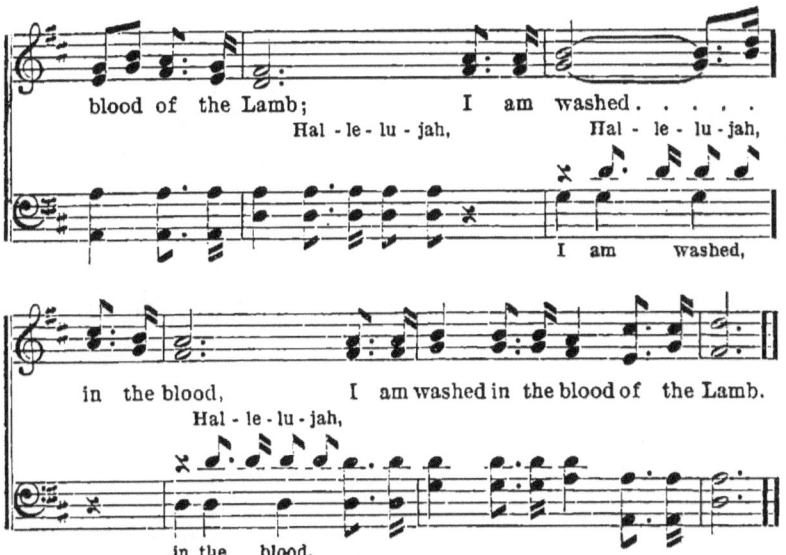

No. 3.   Dennis. S. M.

Rev. John Fawcett.   H. G. Nageli.

1. Blest be the tie that binds Our hearts in Christian love;
2. Before our Father's throne, We pour our ardent pray'rs;
3. We share our mutual woes; Our mutual burdens bear;
4. When we asunder part, It gives us inward pain;

The fellowship of kindred minds Is like to that above.
Our fears, our hopes, our aims are one, Our comforts and our cares.
And often for each other flows The sympathizing tear.
But we shall still be join'd in heart, And hope to meet again.

No. 4. Hark! the Voice of Jesus Calling.

Dr. H. R. Palmer.

1. Hark! the voice of Jesus calling, "Follow me, follow me!"
2. Who will heed the holy mandate, "Follow me, follow me!"
3. Hearken, lest He plead no longer, "Follow me, follow me!"

Softly thro' the silence falling, "Follow, follow me!"
Leaving all things at His bidding, "Follow, follow me!"
Once again, oh, hear Him calling, "Follow, follow me!"

As of old He called the fishers, When he walked by Galilee,
Hark! that tender voice entreating Mariners on life's rough sea,
Turning swift at Thy sweet summons, Evermore, O Christ, would we,

Still His patient voice is pleading, "Follow, follow me!"
Gently, lovingly, repeating, "Follow, follow me!"
For Thy love all else forsaking, Follow, follow Thee!

By permission H. R. Palmer, owner of Copyright.

No. 8. Take Up Thy Cross To-day.

"Let him deny himself, and take up his cross daily, and follow me." Luke ix: 23.

R. L.   Rev. ROBERT LOWRY.
May be sung as a Solo.

1. "Take up thy cross and follow Me," O hear the blessed Saviour say; If thou wouldst His dis-ci-ple be, Take up thy cross to-day.
2. Let not the world thy soul des-troy, When Je-sus shows the bet-ter way; O now be-lieve Him, and with joy Take up thy cross to-day.
3. Behold th'accepted time is now; O flee the danger of de-lay; E-ter-nal life is thine if thou Take up thy cross to-day.

CHORUS.

Take up thy cross to-day, Take up thy cross to-day; ... O
Take up thy cross to-day, Take up thy cross to-day;

rit.

hear thy Lord, and trust His word; Take up thy cross to-day.

No. 9. Near the Cross.

"But God forbid that I should glory, save in the cross of our Lord Jesus Christ." GAL. vi: 14.

E. R. Latta.   J. H. Ruebush.

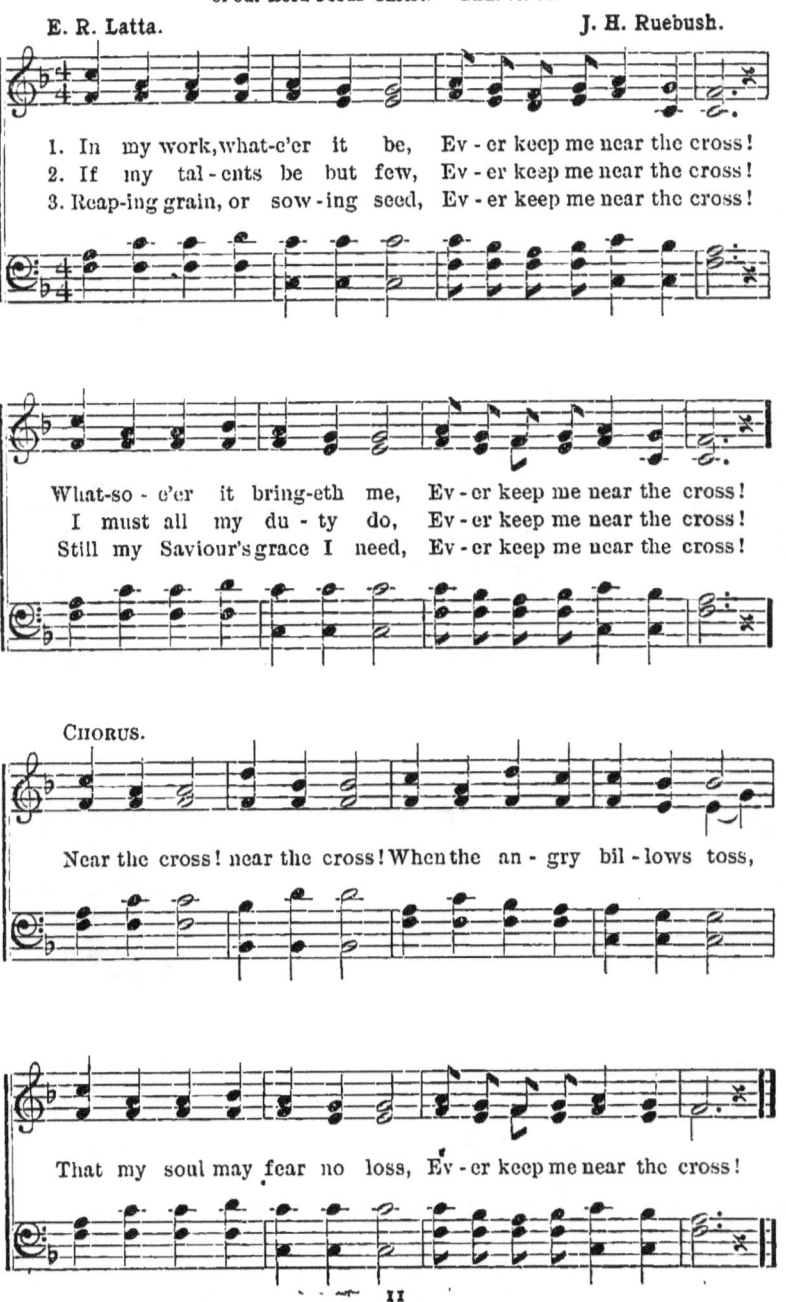

1. In my work, what-e'er it be, Ev-er keep me near the cross!
2. If my tal-ents be but few, Ev-er keep me near the cross!
3. Reap-ing grain, or sow-ing seed, Ev-er keep me near the cross!

What-so-e'er it bring-eth me, Ev-er keep me near the cross!
I must all my du-ty do, Ev-er keep me near the cross!
Still my Saviour's grace I need, Ev-er keep me near the cross!

CHORUS.

Near the cross! near the cross! When the an-gry bil-lows toss,

That my soul may fear no loss, Ev-er keep me near the cross!

No. 10. **Ever Will I Pray.**

Copyright used by permission. From "Shining Light."

No. 11. Happy Spirits.

Rev. J. C. Burkett.

1. Death shall not de-stroy my comfort, Christ shall guide me thro' the gloom;
2. Jor-dan's streams shall not o'er-flow me While my Saviour's by my side;
3. Smil-ing an-gels now surround me, Troops resplendent fill the skies;
4. Je - sus, clad in daz-zling splendor, Now, methinks, appears in view!

Down He'll send some angel con-voy   To con vey my spir-it home.
Ca-naan, Ca-naan lies be-fore me,   Rise, and cross the swelling tide.
Glo - ry shin-ing all a-round me   While my hap-py spir-it flies.
Brethren, could you see my Je - sus, You would love and serve Him, too.

CHORUS.

Soon with an-gels I'll be marching With bright glo-ry on my brow;

Who will share my blissful portion, Who will love my Saviour now?

By permission.

No. 12. Do They Pray for Me at Home?

J. H. Tenney.

Do They Pray for Me at Home? Concluded.

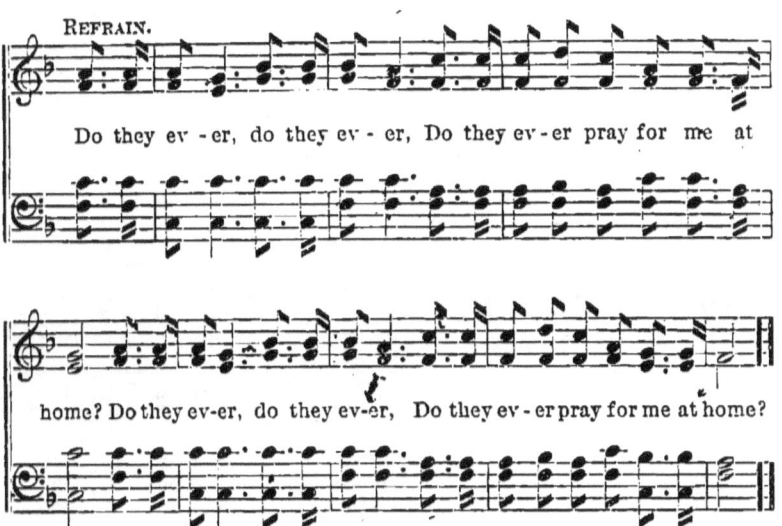

No. 13. I am Coming to the Cross.

Rev. W. McDonald.   Wm. G. Fischer. By per.

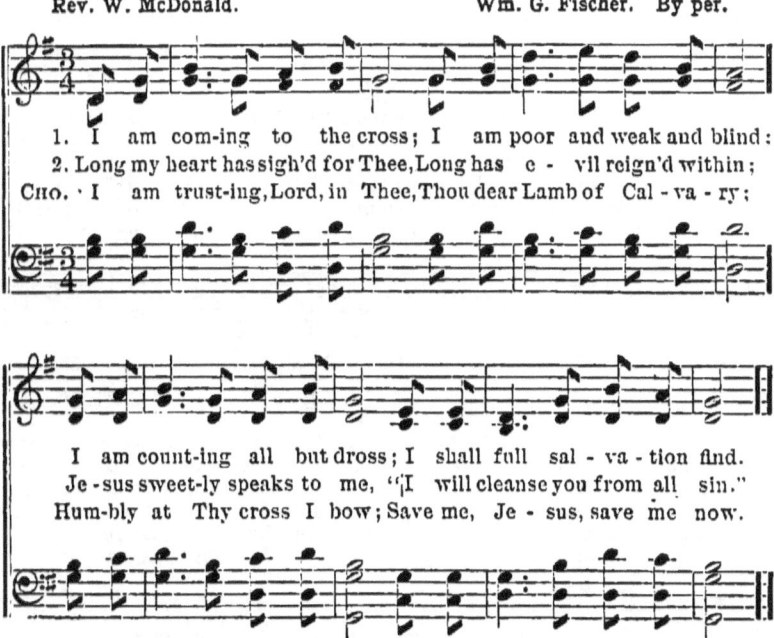

No. 17. At the Beautiful Gate.

Rev. J. H. Martin. R. M. McIntosh. By per.

3 O Lord, I beseech Thee for
  wisdom and grace,
In winning lost souls unto Thee,
That many may be in that
  beautiful place,
A crown of rejoicing to me.

No. 18.   Hosanna

Copyright, 1882, by Hugg & Armstrong.

No. 20. **Marching in the Light.**

J. B. M. J. B. Moon. By per.

From "Gospel Voice."

Marching in the Light. Concluded.

No. 21. How Sweet, How Heavenly.

Wm. B. Bradbury.

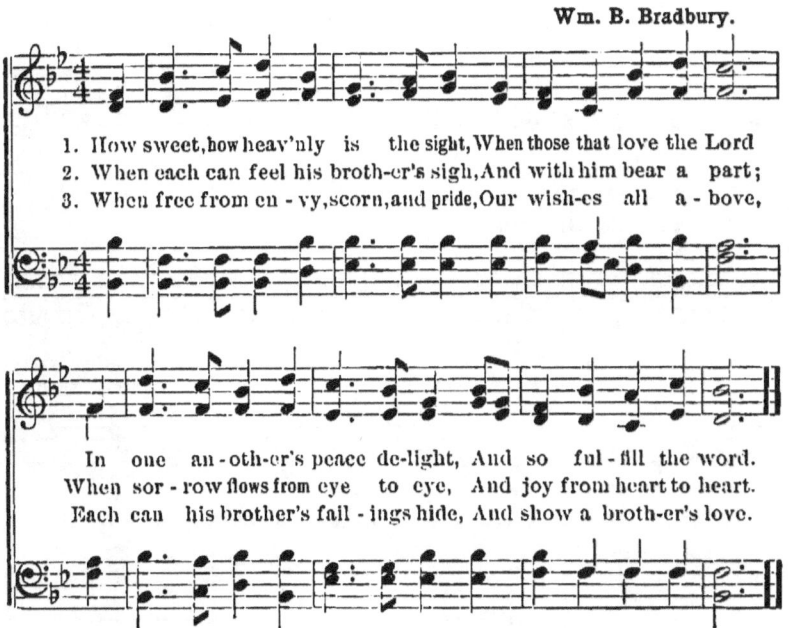

1. How sweet, how heav'nly is the sight, When those that love the Lord
2. When each can feel his broth-er's sigh, And with him bear a part;
3. When free from en-vy, scorn, and pride, Our wish-es all a-bove,

In one an-oth-er's peace de-light, And so ful-fill the word.
When sor-row flows from eye to eye, And joy from heart to heart.
Each can his brother's fail-ings hide, And show a broth-er's love.

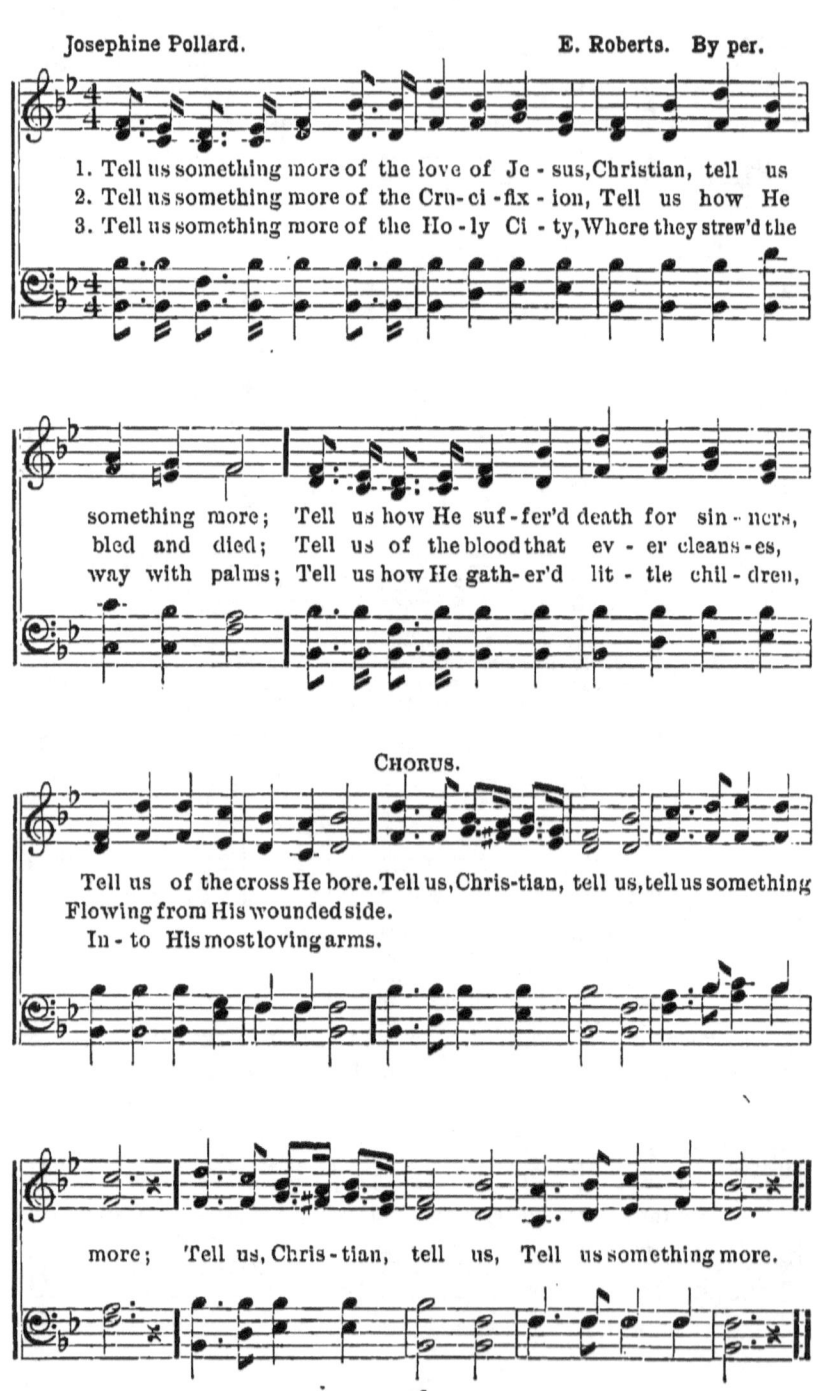

No. 26. God's Hand Doth Lead Me On.

Jas. H. Ruebush.

1. 'Tis God's own hand that lead-eth me A-long my pil-grim way, But not be-cause He need-eth me, I need Him for my stay.
2. 'Tis God's own hand that lead-eth me A-long my toil-some way; And since in love He feed-eth me, I'll trust Him day by day.
3. 'Tis God's own hand that lead-eth me A-long my wea-ry way; And ev-'ry day He speed-eth me, To-ward e-ter-nal day.

REFRAIN.

So God's own hand doth lead me on Thro' darkness and thro' gloom, And well I know where e'er I go His hand will lead me home.

No. 32. Jesus, I My Cross Have Taken.

"Having made peace through the blood of His cross." Col. i: 20.

J. H. Ruebush.

Jesus, I My Cross have Taken. Concluded.

di - - tion, God and heav'n are still my own.
rich is my con-di-tion, God and heav'n are still my own.

No. 33. Forever Here My Rest.

"My flesh shall rest in hope." Acts ii: 26.

J. H. Hall.

1. For-ev-er here my rest shall be, Close to Thy bleed-ing side;
2. No voice can sing, no heart can frame, Nor can the mem-'ry find
3. O, hope of ev-'ry con-trite heart, O, joy of all the meek!

This all my hope and all my plea; For me the Sav-iour died.
A sweet-er sound than Je - sus' name—The Sav-iour of man-kind.
To those who ask, how kind Thou art, How good to those who seek!

For me, for me, What can I ask be - side?
Dear name, dear name, No oth-er can I find;
How good, how good, How good to those who seek;

For me, for me,
Dear name, dear name,
How good, how good,

By permission. Copyright, 1892, by R. L. Selle.

No. 34. Battle Hymn.

Rev. I. Watts, D.D.   English. Arr. by Wm. B. Blake.

1. Am I a soldier of the cross, A fol-l'wer of the Lamb,
And shall I fear to own His cause, Or blush to speak His name?
2. Must I be carried to the skies On flow'ry beds of ease,
While others fought to win the prize, And sail'd thro' bloody seas?

CHORUS.
And when the battle's over we shall wear a crown! Yes, we shall wear a crown! Yes, we shall wear a crown! And when the battle's over we shall wear a crown In the new Jerusalem.

Wear a crown, wear a crown, Wear a bright and shining crown;
Wear a crown, wear a crown,

3. Are there no foes for me to face?
Must I not stem the flood?
Is this vile world a friend to grace
To help me on to God?

4. Sure I must fight if I would reign,
Increase my courage, Lord;
I'll bear the toil, endure the pain,
Supported by Thy word.

No. 35. **Jesus, I My Cross have Taken.**

Henry Francis Lyte, 1824.

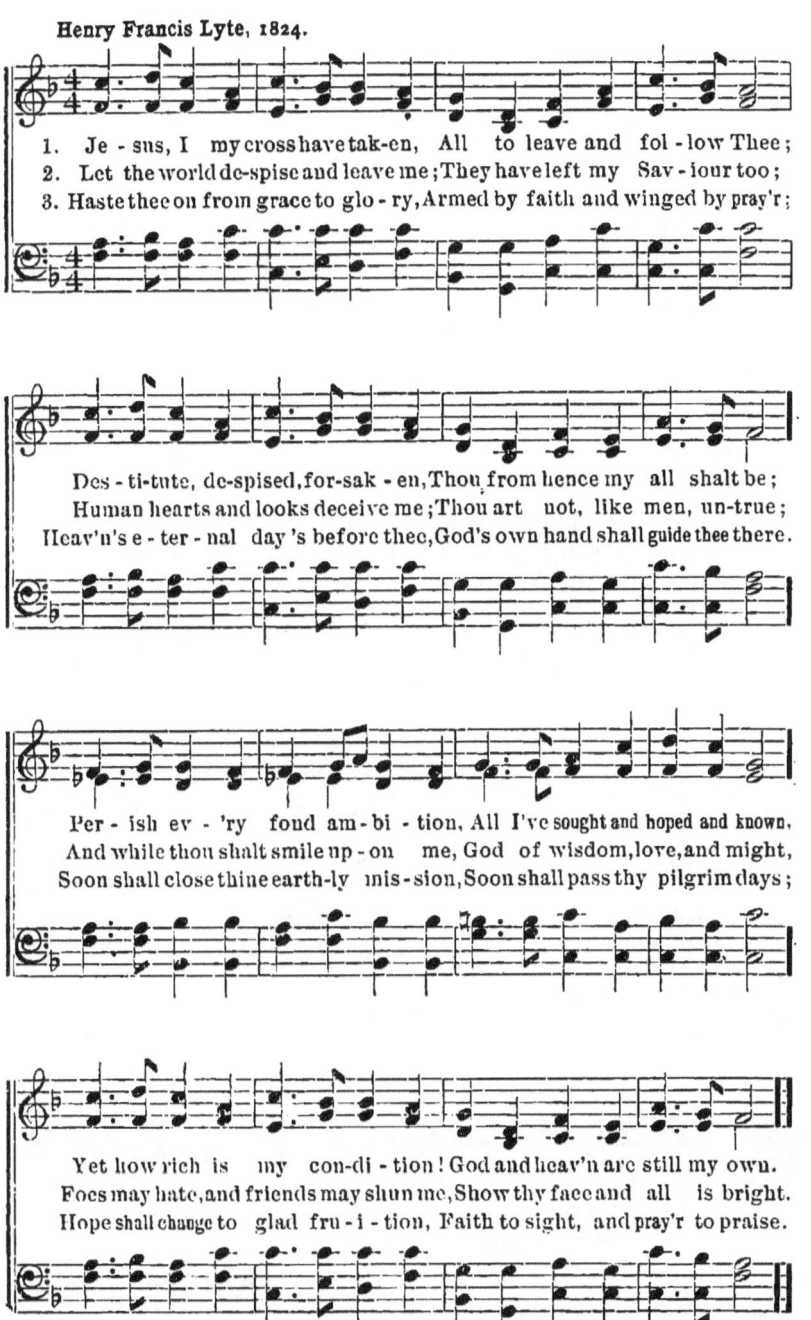

1. Je-sus, I my cross have tak-en, All to leave and fol-low Thee;
2. Let the world de-spise and leave me; They have left my Sav-iour too;
3. Haste thee on from grace to glo-ry, Armed by faith and winged by pray'r;

Des-ti-tute, de-spised, for-sak-en, Thou from hence my all shalt be;
Human hearts and looks deceive me; Thou art not, like men, un-true;
Heav'n's e-ter-nal day's before thee, God's own hand shall guide thee there.

Per-ish ev-'ry fond am-bi-tion, All I've sought and hoped and known,
And while thou shalt smile up-on me, God of wisdom, love, and might,
Soon shall close thine earth-ly mis-sion, Soon shall pass thy pilgrim days;

Yet how rich is my con-di-tion! God and heav'n are still my own.
Foes may hate, and friends may shun me, Show thy face and all is bright.
Hope shall change to glad fru-i-tion, Faith to sight, and pray'r to praise.

No. 36.   I Want to Be a Worker.

I. Baltzell. By per.

1. I want to be a work-er for the Lord, I want to love and
2. I want to be a work-er ev-'ry day, I want to lead the
3. I want to be a work-er strong and brave, I want to trust in
4. I want to be a work-er, help me, Lord, To lead the lost and

trust His ho-ly word, I want to sing and pray, and be
err-ing in the way That leads to heav'n a-bove, where
Je-sus' pow'r to save, All who will tru-ly come, shall
err-ing to Thy word, That points to joys on high, where

bus-y ev-'ry day In the vine-yard of the Lord.
all is peace and love, In the king-dom of the Lord.
find a hap-py home, In the king-dom of the Lord.
pleas-ures nev-er die, In the king-dom of the Lord.

CHORUS.

I will work, I will pray, In the vineyard, in the
I will work and pray, I will work and pray,

I Want to Be a Worker. Concluded.

No. 37. Rock of Ages.

1. Je-sus, Lov-er of my soul, Let me to Thy bos-om fly,
2. Oth-er ref-uge have I none: Hangs my helpless soul on Thee:
3. All my trust on Thee is stayed; All my help from Thee I bring;

REF. Rock of A-ges, cleft for me, Rock of A-ges, cleft for me,

D.C. for Ref.

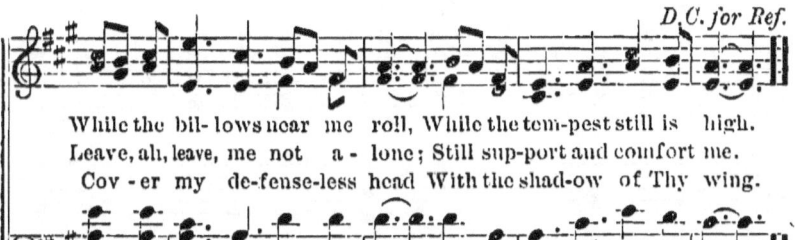

While the bil-lows near me roll, While the tem-pest still is high.
Leave, ah, leave, me not a-lone; Still sup-port and comfort me.
Cov-er my de-fense-less head With the shad-ow of Thy wing.

Rock of A-ges, cleft for me, Let me hide my-self in Thee.

Title Clear. Concluded.

3 Let cares, like a wild deluge come,
  Let storms of sorrow fall;
  So I but safely reach my home,
  My God, my heaven, my all.

4 There I shall bathe my weary soul
  In seas of heavenly rest,
  And not a wave of trouble roll
  Across my peaceful breast.

No. 39. Safe at Home.

Rev. W. F. Cosner. W. T. Dale. By per.

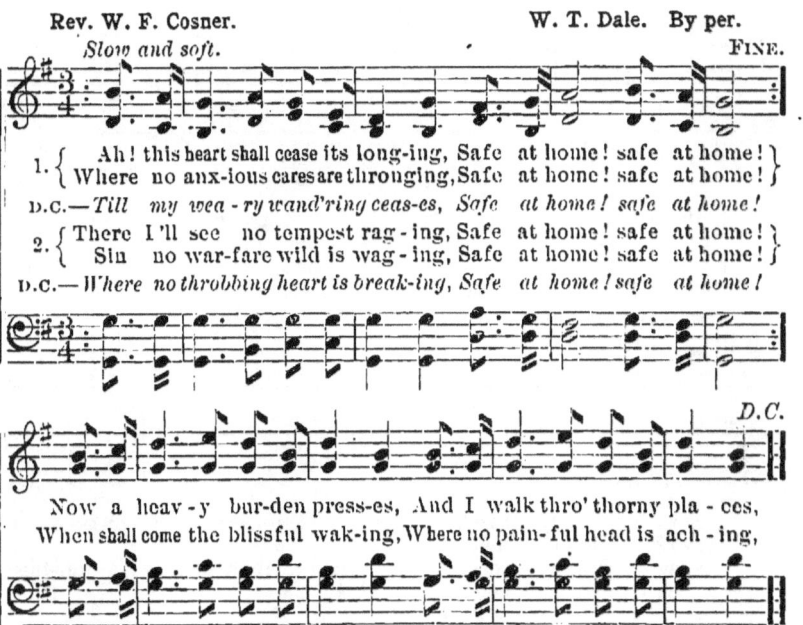

3 There are friends who with me parted,
  Safe at home! safe at home!
  No more wand'ring broken hearted,
  Safe at home! safe at home!
  Undisturb'd while storms are sweeping,
  Calmly now the loved are sleeping,
  Ever in their Father's keeping,
  Safe at home! safe at home!

4 Dear ones gone before will meet me,
  Safe at home! safe at home!
  At the pearly gate will greet me,
  Safe at home! safe at home!
  Saviour, dearest Saviour, hear me,
  I am weary, be Thou near me,
  Oh, sustain me till Thou cheer me,
  Safe at home! safe at home!

Copyright, 1885, by W. T. Dale.

No. 41. We'll Work Till Jesus Comes.

"Thy work shall be rewarded." Jer. xxxi: 17.

Mrs. Elizabeth Mills.   Dr. Wm. Miller.

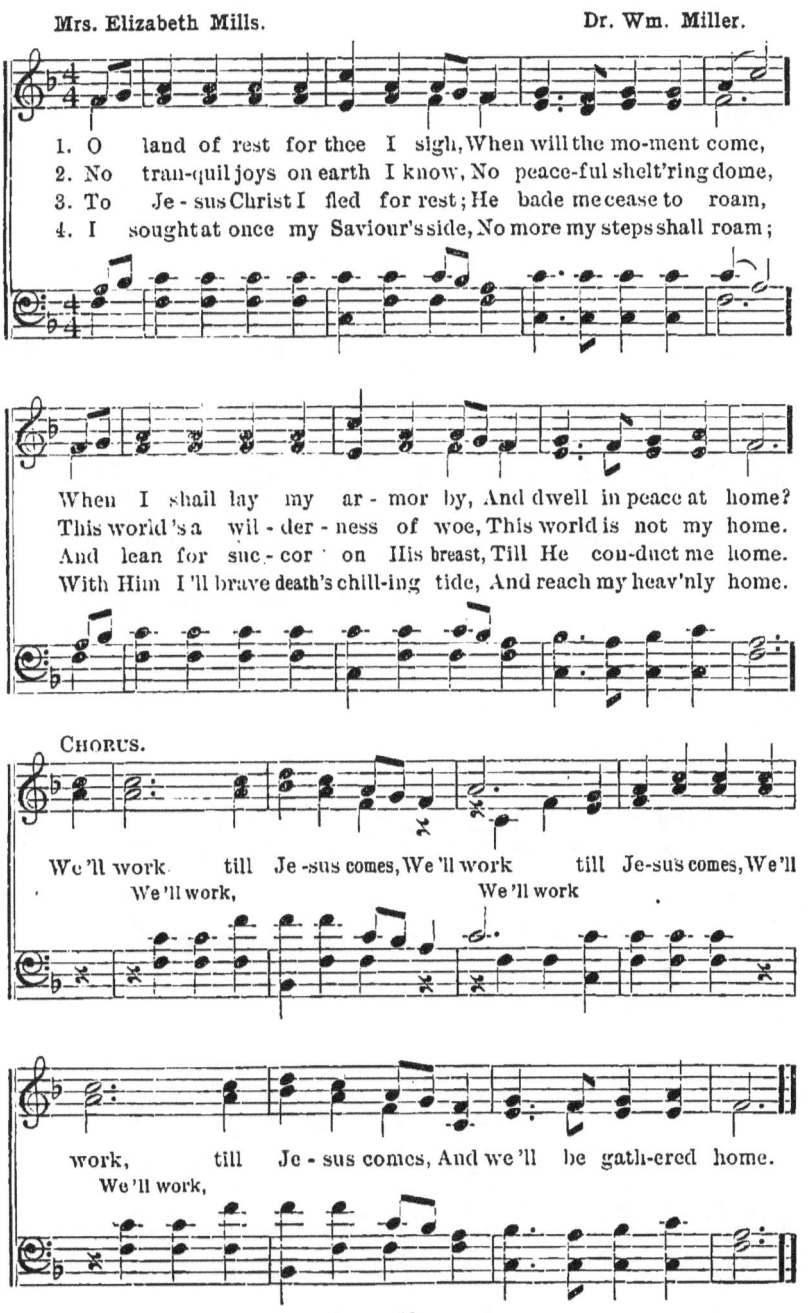

1. O land of rest for thee I sigh, When will the moment come,
2. No tranquil joys on earth I know, No peaceful shelt'ring dome,
3. To Jesus Christ I fled for rest; He bade me cease to roam,
4. I sought at once my Saviour's side, No more my steps shall roam;

When I shall lay my armor by, And dwell in peace at home?
This world's a wilderness of woe, This world is not my home.
And lean for succor on His breast, Till He conduct me home.
With Him I'll brave death's chilling tide, And reach my heav'nly home.

CHORUS.

We'll work till Jesus comes, We'll work till Jesus comes, We'll
We'll work,   We'll work

work, till Jesus comes, And we'll be gathered home.
We'll work,

No. 43.　　　　**Under His Wings.**

Asa Hull. By per.

3　The pestilence walking about,
　　When darkness has settled abroad,
　　Can never compel me to doubt
　　The presence and power of God.

4　The wasting destruction at noon,
　　No fearful foreboding can bring;
　　With Jesus, my soul doth commune,
　　His perfect salvation I sing.

5　A thousand may fall at my side,
　　Ten thousand upon my right hand;
　　Above me His wings are spread wide,
　　Beneath them in safety I stand.

Let Me Rest. Concluded.

CHORUS.

In the shad-ow of the Rock let me rest, In the shad-ow of the Rock let me rest; When I feel the tem-pest's shock thrill my breast, . . . In the shadow of the Rock let me rest.
thrill my breast,

No. 45. Lottie.

Philip Doddridge.   W. B. Bradbury.

1. How gen-tle God's com-mands, How kind His pre-cepts are;
2. His boun-ty will pro-vide, His saints se-cure-ly dwell;
3. His good-ness stands ap-proved Thro' each suc-ceed-ing day;

Come, cast your bur-den on the Lord, And trust His con-stant care.
That hand which bears cre - a - tion up, Shall guard His chil-dren well.
I'll drop my bur-den at His feet, And bear a song a - way.

No. 47. **The Banquet of Love.**

A. S. Kieffer. A. S. Kieffer.

No. 49. I was a Wandering Sheep.

Horatius Bonar.   Rev. D. C. John.

1. I was a wand'ring sheep, I did not love the fold; I did not love my Shepherd's voice, I would not be con-troll'd: I was a way-ward child, I did not love my home; I did not love my Fa-ther's voice, I lov'd a-far to roam.
2. The Shepherd sought His sheep, The Fa-ther sought His child; He fol-low'd me o'er vale and hill, O'er des-ert waste and wild; He found me nigh to death, De-spair-ing, faint, and lone; He bound me with the bonds of love, He sav'd the wand'ring one.
3. Je-sus my Shep-herd is, 'Twas He that sav'd my soul; 'Twas He that wash'd me in His blood, 'Twas He that made me whole; 'Twas He that sought the lost, That found the wand'ring sheep; 'T was He that bro't me to the fold, 'T is He that still doth keep.
4. No more a wand'ring sheep, I long to be con-troll'd; I love my ten-der Shepherd's voice, I love the peace-ful fold; No more a way-ward child, I seek no more to roam; I love my heav'n-ly Fa-ther's voice, I love, I love His home.

Copyright, 1893, by Rev. D. C. John. By permission.

Wandering Home. Concluded.

oth-er at last, At home on "the heav-en-ly shore."

No. 51.   Nearer the Cross.

"The cross of our Lord Jesus Christ." Gal. vi: 14.

Charlotte Abbey.   J. H. Hall.

1. Near-er the cross of Je-sus, Ev-er let me be;
2. Near-er the cross of Je-sus, There I would a-bide;
3. Near-er the cross of Je-sus, Let me live and die;

Near-er the flow-ing foun-tain, That cleans-eth me.
There let me rest for-ev-er, Near Je-sus' side.
There I will find sweet ref-uge, And safe-ty nigh.

D.S. Near-er the flow-ing foun-tain, That cleans-eth me.

CHORUS.

Near-er the cross, Near-er the cross, Near-er the cross of Je-sus.

Copyright, 1894, by J. H. Hall.

No. 53.   **The Child of a King.**

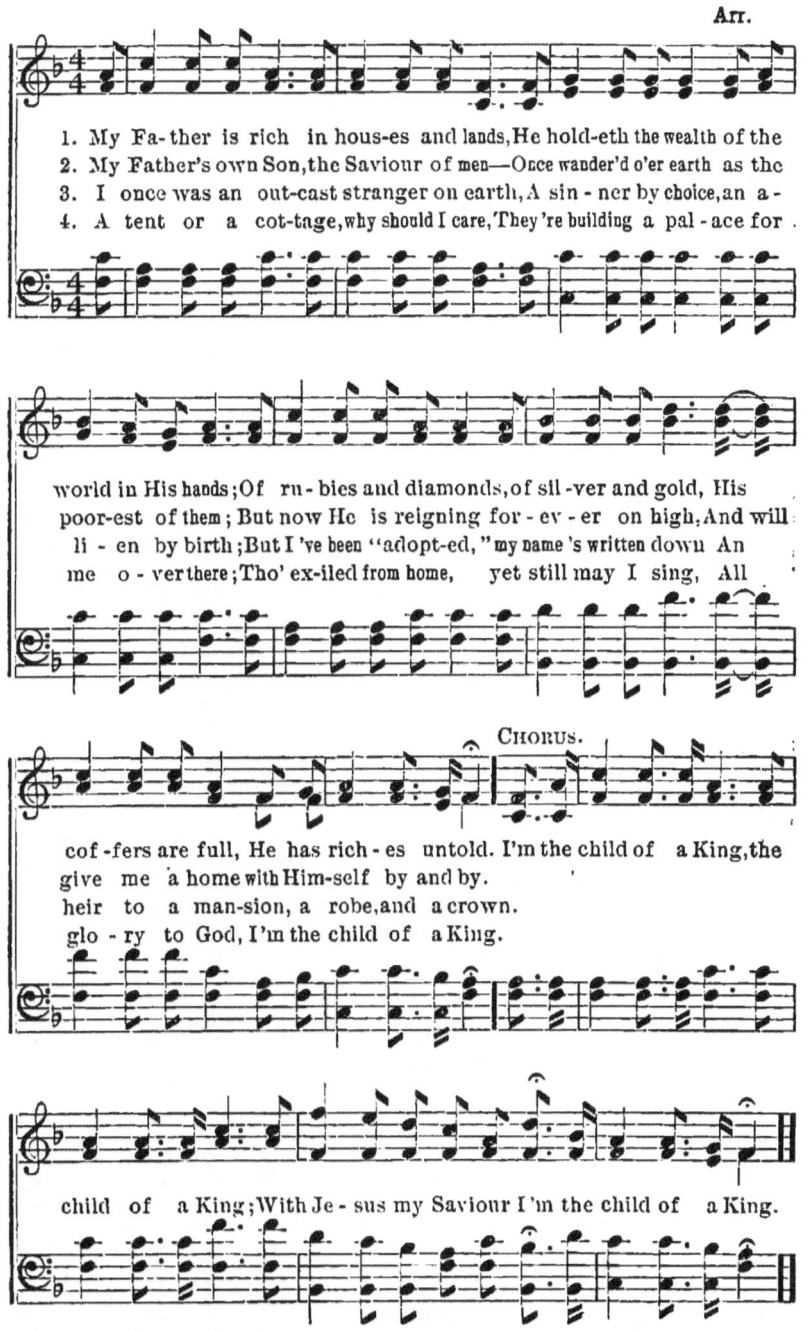

1. My Father is rich in houses and lands, He holdeth the wealth of the world in His hands; Of rubies and diamonds, of silver and gold, His coffers are full, He has riches untold.
2. My Father's own Son, the Saviour of men—Once wander'd o'er earth as the poorest of them; But now He is reigning forever on high, And will give me a home with Himself by and by.
3. I once was an outcast stranger on earth, A sinner by choice, an alien by birth; But I've been "adopted," my name's written down An heir to a mansion, a robe, and a crown.
4. A tent or a cottage, why should I care, They're building a palace for me over there; Tho' exiled from home, yet still may I sing, All glory to God, I'm the child of a King.

CHORUS.

I'm the child of a King, the child of a King; With Jesus my Saviour I'm the child of a King.

Why Stand Ye Here Idle? Concluded.

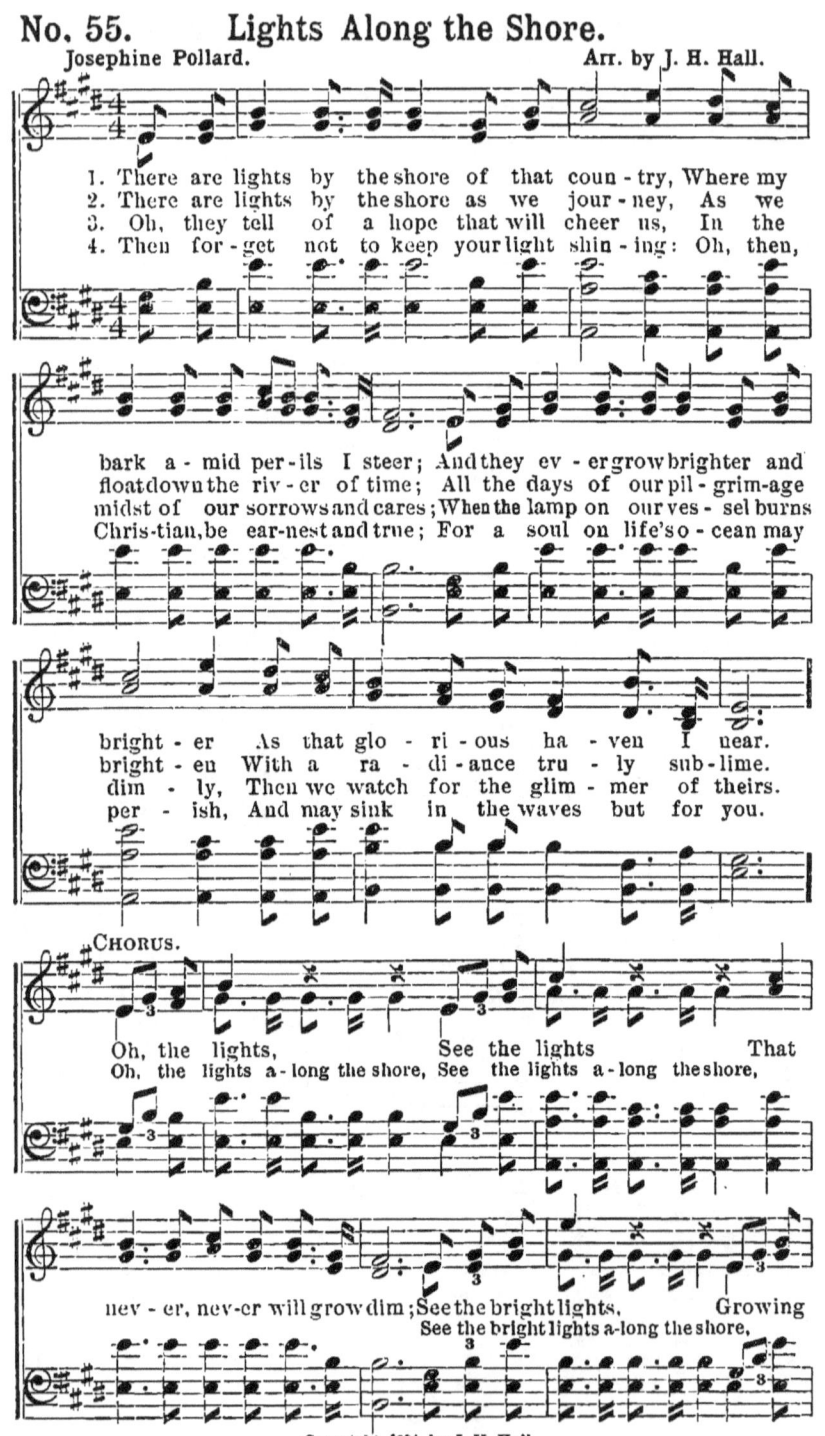

Lights Along the Shore. Concluded.

bright - er, And they guide us un - to Him.
brighter, ev - er bright-er, And they guide us, yes, they guide us un-to Him.

No. 56. Revive Us Again.

Dr. W. Mackay. English Melody.

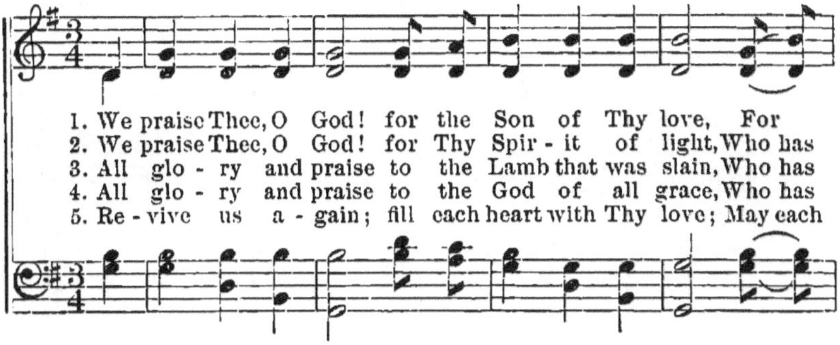

1. We praise Thee, O God! for the Son of Thy love, For
2. We praise Thee, O God! for Thy Spir - it of light, Who has
3. All glo - ry and praise to the Lamb that was slain, Who has
4. All glo - ry and praise to the God of all grace, Who has
5. Re - vive us a - gain; fill each heart with Thy love; May each

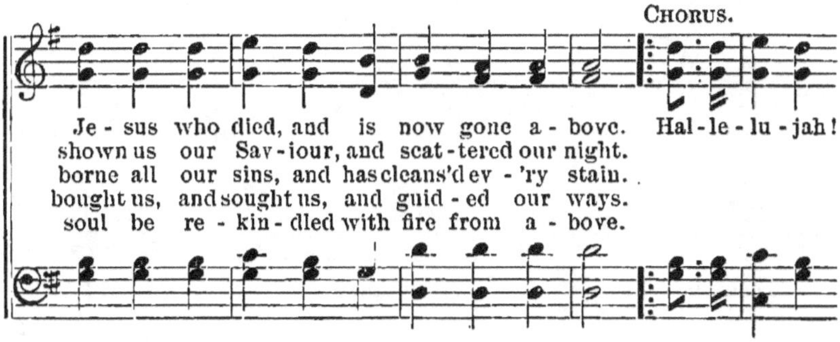

CHORUS.

Je - sus who died, and is now gone a - bove. Hal - le - lu - jah!
shown us our Sav - iour, and scat - tered our night.
borne all our sins, and has cleans'd ev - 'ry stain.
bought us, and sought us, and guid - ed our ways.
soul be re - kin - dled with fire from a - bove.

Thine the glo - ry, Hal - le - lu - jah! A - men. Re - vive us a - gain.

Lead Me On. Concluded.

on, To the realms of end-less day.
lead me on,

No. 58. Holy Spirit, Faithful Guide.

"I will guide thee with mine eyes." Ps. xxxii: 8.

M. M. W.   M. M. Wells.

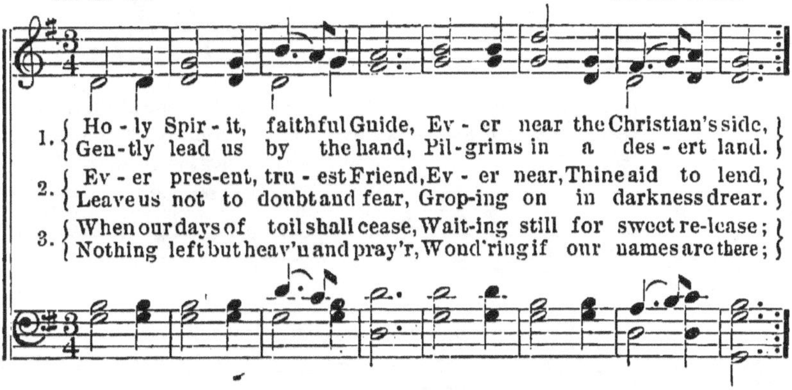

1. { Ho-ly Spir-it, faithful Guide, Ev-er near the Christian's side, }
   { Gen-tly lead us by the hand, Pil-grims in a des-ert land. }
2. { Ev-er pres-ent, tru-est Friend, Ev-er near, Thine aid to lend, }
   { Leave us not to doubt and fear, Grop-ing on in darkness drear. }
3. { When our days of toil shall cease, Wait-ing still for sweet re-lease; }
   { Nothing left but heav'n and pray'r, Wond'ring if our names are there; }

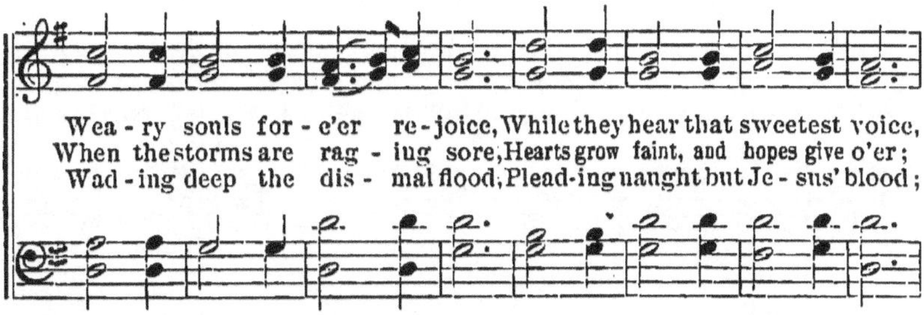

Wea-ry souls for-e'er re-joice, While they hear that sweetest voice,
When the storms are rag-ing sore, Hearts grow faint, and hopes give o'er;
Wad-ing deep the dis-mal flood, Plead-ing naught but Je-sus' blood;

Whisp'ring soft-ly, wan-d'rer come! Fol-low me, I'll guide thee home.

Sowing Time. Concluded.

No. 61. Go and Inquire.

"Search the scriptures, for in them ye think ye have eternal life." John v: 39.

W. A. O.
W. A. Ogden.

By permission.

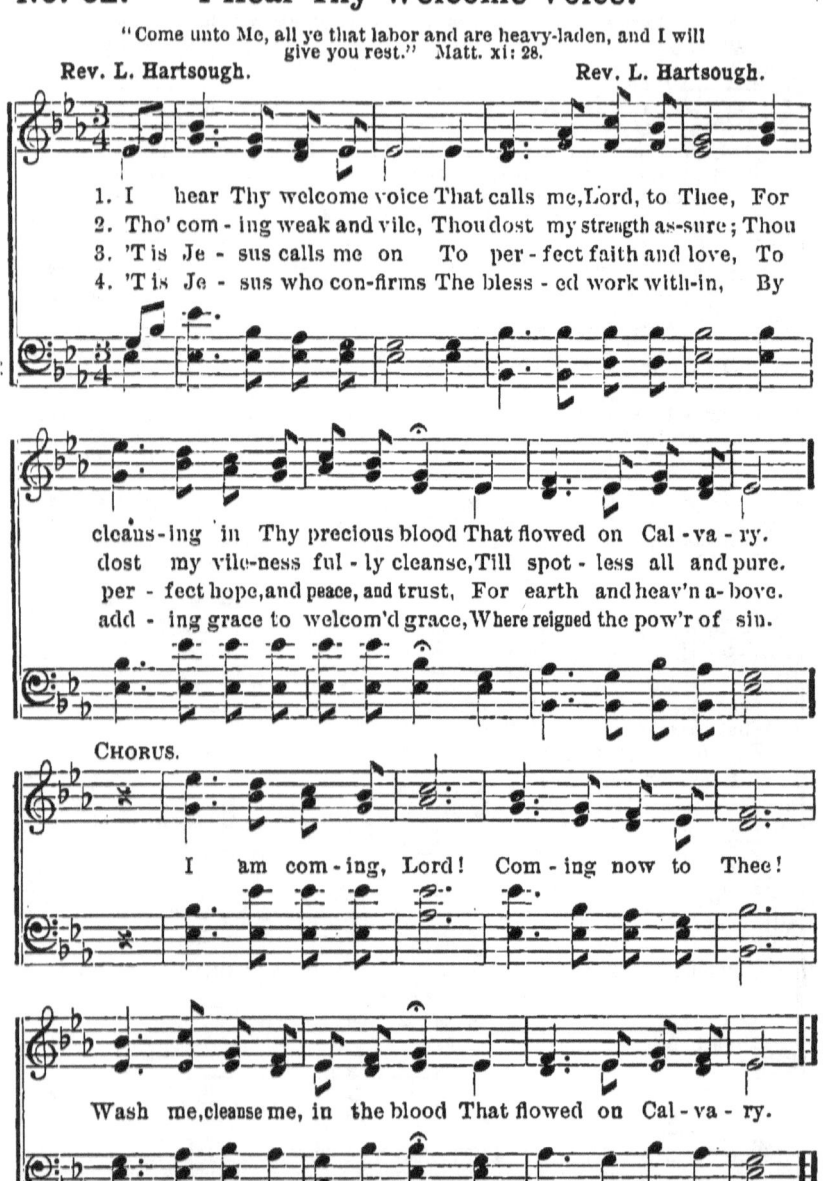

No. 63. The Heavenly Crown.

"Ye shall receive a crown of glory that fadeth not away." 1 Peter v: 4.

Anon.   J. H. Hall.

1. Gra-cious Sav-iour, can it be There a-waits a crown for me,
2. Can it be a harp of gold, Glitt'ring bright, these hands shall hold?
3. Shall I pass the pearl-y gates? Shall I walk the gold-en streets?

Set with gems so pure, so bright, Sparkling each with heav'nly light?
That this voice shall join the song, Sung by an-gels round the throne?
Shall I see the great white throne, And be-hold the Lamb thereon?

CHORUS.

Yes, oh, yes, if you believe, Je - - - sus
Yes, if you be-lieve,   Je-sus has a crown,

has a crown to give; Yes,   oh,
                 Yes, if you be-lieve,

yes, if you be-lieve, Je - sus has a crown to give.

Copyright, 1894, by J. H. Hall.

It May be the Last. Concluded.

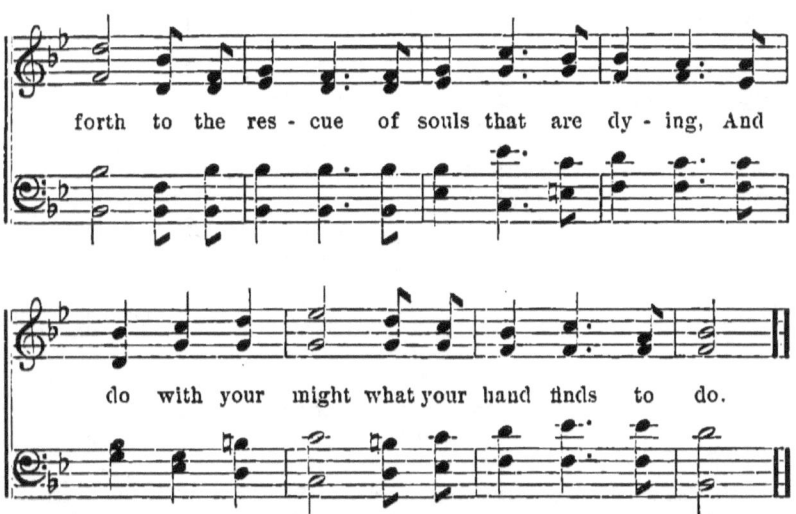

forth to the res-cue of souls that are dy-ing, And
do with your might what your hand finds to do.

No. 65. Arlington.

Dr. Arne.

1. Once more we come be-fore our God; Once more His bless-ings ask:
2. Fa-ther, Thy quick-'ning Spir-it send From heav'n in Je-sus' name,
3. May we re-ceive the word we hear, Each in an hon-est heart;
4. To seek Thee all our hearts dispose, To each Thy blessings suit,

O may not du-ty seem a load, Nor wor-ship seem a task!
To make our wait-ing minds at-tend, And put our souls in frame.
And keep the pre-cious treas-ure there, And nev-er with it part.
And let the seed Thy ser-vant sows Pro-duce a-bun-dant fruit.

No. 66. When the Shining Gates Unfold.

Laura E. Newell.   J. H. Ruebush.

By permission.

When the Shining Gates Unfold. Concluded.

No. 67. Come to Jesus.

2 He will save you, etc.
3 Oh, believe Him.
4 He is able.
5 He is willing.
6 He'll receive you.
7 Call upon Him.
8 He will hear you.
9 Look unto Him.
10 He'll forgive you.
11 Don't reject Him.
12 Jesus loves you.
13 Only trust Him.

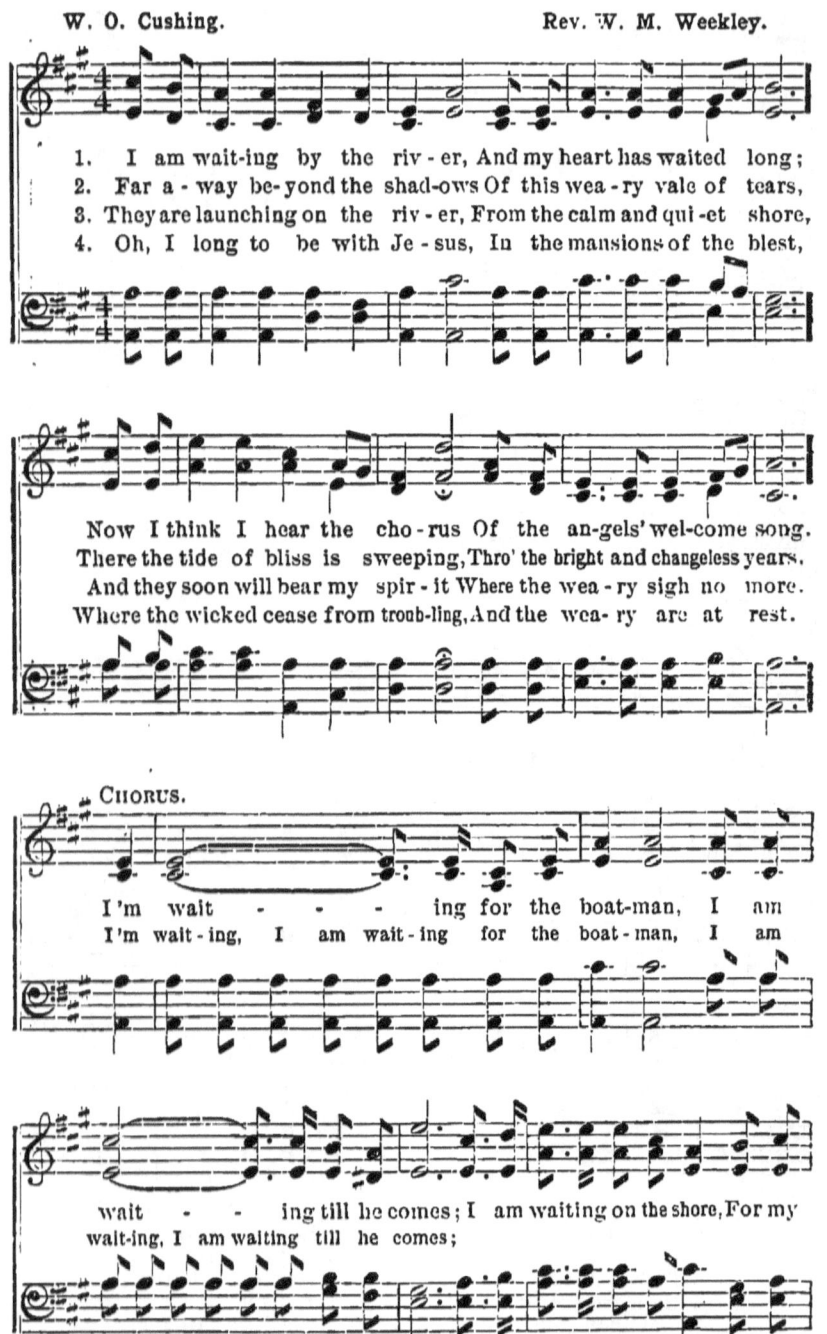

No. 71. **Hiding in the Rock.**

By permission.

No. 74. What Shall Our Record Be.

Solo and Chorus.

F. M. D. Frank M. Davis.

1. There's a hand that's writing now In the book of life, they say; Ev-'ry
2. Still that hand goes writing on, Mak-ing pa-ges dark or fair; Let us
3. Time is eb-bing fast a-way, Life for us will soon be done; Can we,

ac-tion, word or deed Is re-cord-ed there each day. What shall then our record be? Let us
ponder well, dear friend, What for us is written there.
trusting-ly, go hence, That a crown of life is won.

stop and think, I pray! What shall then our record be, In the coming judgment day?

By per. Frank M. Davis, owner of copyright.

The Unclouded Day. Concluded.

home where no storm-clouds rise, O they tell me of an uncloud-ed day.
friends by the tree of life, In the land of the uncloud-ed day.
King and His snow-white throne, In the land of the uncloud-ed day.
beau-ty in-vites me there, To the land of the uncloud-ed day.

No. 77. Nearer, My God, to Thee.

Dr. Lowell Mason.

1. Near-er, my God, to Thee, Near-er to Thee; E'en tho' it
2. Tho' like a wan-der-er, Day-light all gone, Dark-ness be
3. There let the way ap-pear Steps up to heav'n; All that Thou

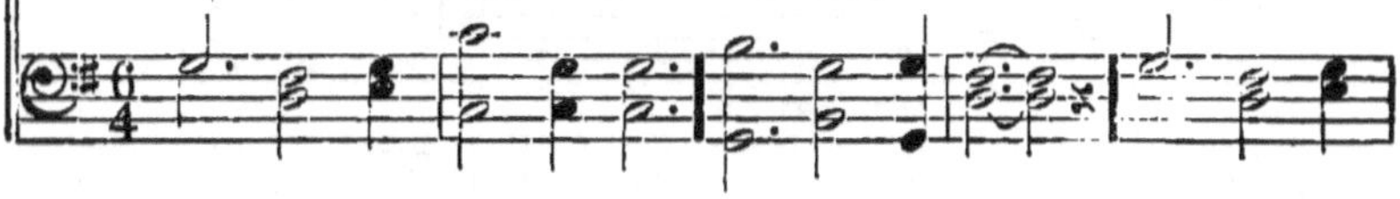

be a cross That rais-eth me; Still all my song shall be,
o-ver me, My rest a stone; Yet in my dreams I'd be,
send-est me In mer-cy giv'n; An-gels to beck-on me

Nearer, my God, to Thee, Nearer, my God, to Thee, Near-er to Thee.

No. 78. What a Glorious Redeemer!

Rev. H. G. Jackson.   A. Beirly.

1. My Saviour left His throne on high, And came on earth for me to die;
2. Beneath the heavy cross, low bent, Up Calv'ry's rugged steeps He went;
3. That all might know His pow'r to save, He rose in triumph from the grave;
4. Reign too, O blessed King divine, Forever in this heart of mine;

What a glorious Redeemer! At midnight in Gethsemane,
What a glorious Redeemer! From sin and death to set me free,
What a glorious Redeemer! And now His cruel suff'rings o'er,
What a glorious Redeemer! Thy sov'reign right in me I own;

He drank the bitter cup for me; What a glorious Redeemer!
There on the cross He died for me; What a glorious Redeemer!
He reigns in bliss for evermore; What a glorious Redeemer!
In life or death I'm Thine alone; What a glorious Redeemer!

CHORUS.

What a glorious Redeemer is Jesus, my Saviour!

What a glorious Redeemer is Jesus, my Lord!

Copyright, 1892, by W. S. Nickle, 108 Washington St., Chicago, Ill.

I am Resting in the Saviour's Love. Concluded.

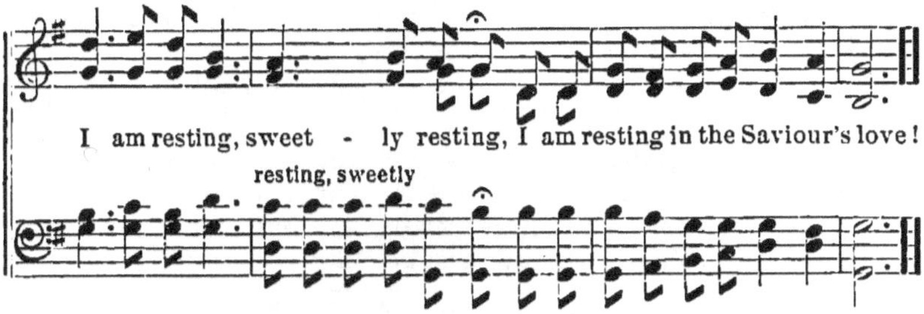
I am resting, sweet - ly resting, I am resting in the Saviour's love!
resting, sweetly

No. 81. Nothing but the Blood of Jesus.

Rev. R. Lowry. Rev. R. Lowry. By per.

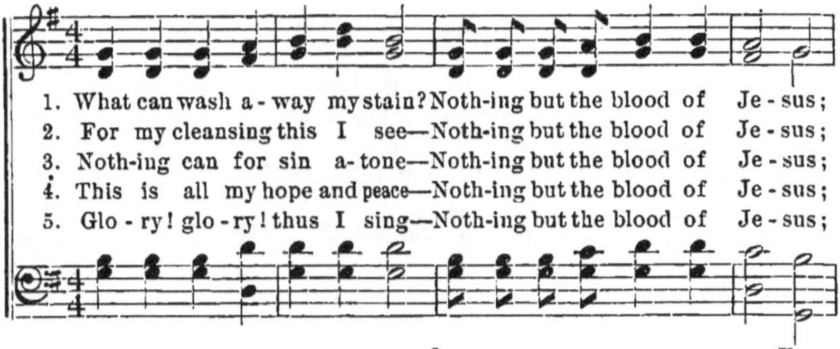
1. What can wash a - way my stain? Noth-ing but the blood of Je - sus;
2. For my cleansing this I see—Noth-ing but the blood of Je - sus;
3. Noth-ing can for sin a - tone—Noth-ing but the blood of Je - sus;
4. This is all my hope and peace—Noth-ing but the blood of Je - sus;
5. Glo - ry! glo - ry! thus I sing—Noth-ing but the blood of Je - sus;

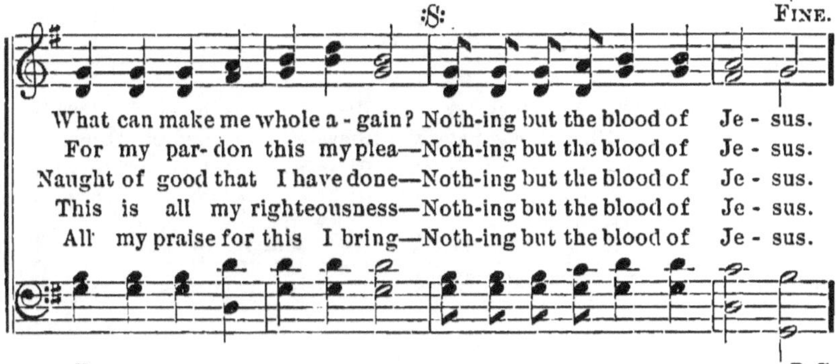
FINE.
What can make me whole a - gain? Noth-ing but the blood of Je - sus.
For my par- don this my plea—Noth-ing but the blood of Je - sus.
Naught of good that I have done—Noth-ing but the blood of Je - sus.
This is all my righteousness—Noth-ing but the blood of Je - sus.
All my praise for this I bring—Noth-ing but the blood of Je - sus.

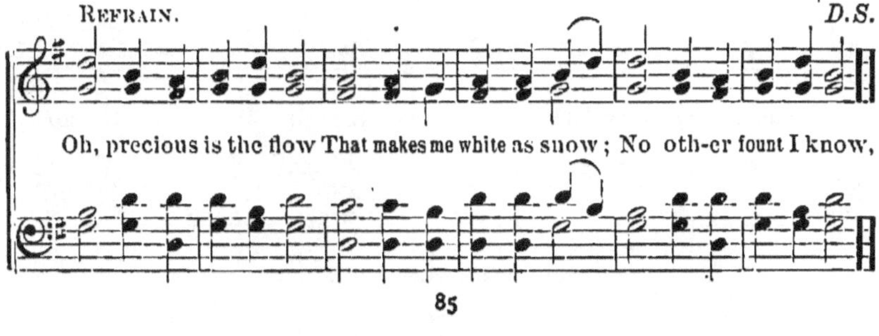
REFRAIN.
D.S.
Oh, precious is the flow That makes me white as snow; No oth-er fount I know,

No. 82. Mercy for All.

Words by Fanny Crosby.   G. P. Benjamin.

1. We are bought with a price by the Lamb that was slain; He has conquer'd the grave—He liv-eth a-gain! At the foot of the cross He will an-swer our call: Bless-ed be the Lord! there is mer-cy for all!
2. We may drink if we will of the foun-tain so free, That is flow-ing to-day for you and for me; With our bur-den of sin at its brink we may fall: Bless-ed be the Lord! there is mer-cy for all!
3. O the rich-es of grace that in Je-sus abound! With the full-ness of joy His peo-ple are crown'd. At the door of His love He will an-swer our call: Bless-ed be the Lord! there is mer-cy for all!
4. If we walk in the path that our Mas-ter has trod,—If we die un-to sin, but live un-to God, When we pass the dark vale He will an-swer our call: Bless-ed be the Lord! there is mer-cy for all!

REFRAIN. Mer-cy for all! Mer-cy for all!

By permission of Biglow & Main, N. Y.

Mercy for All. Concluded.

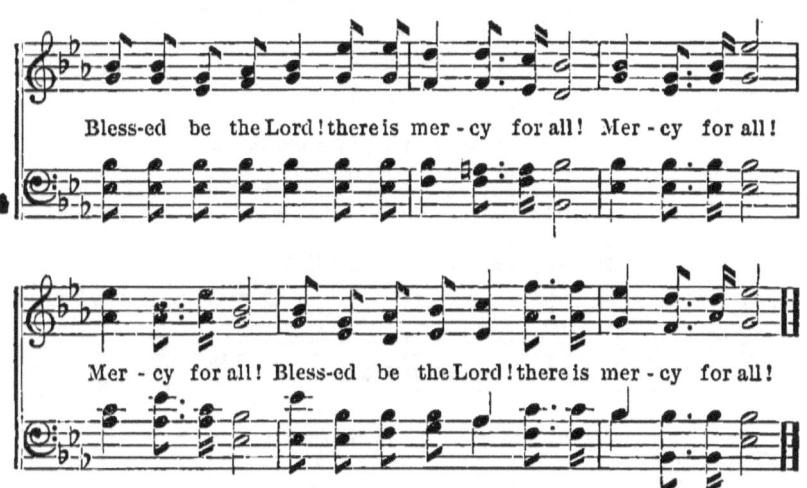

Bless-ed be the Lord! there is mer-cy for all! Mer-cy for all!
Mer-cy for all! Bless-ed be the Lord! there is mer-cy for all!

No. 83. Just as I Am.

Charlotte Elliot.   Wm. B. Bradbury.

1. Just as I am! with-out one plea, But that Thy blood was shed for me,
2. Just as I am! and wait-ing not To rid my soul of one dark blot;
3. Just as I am! tho' toss'd a-bout With many a con-flict, many a doubt,
4. Just as I am! poor, wretch-ed, blind. Sight, rich-es, heal-ing of the mind,
5. Just as I am! Thou wilt re-ceive, Wilt wel-come, pardon, cleanse, re-lieve,

And that Thou bid'st me come to Thee, O Lamb of God! I come, I come!
To Thee, whose blood can cleanse each spot, O Lamb of God! I come, I come!
Fight-ings and fears with-in, with-out, O Lamb of God! I come, I come!
Yea, all I need in Thee to find, O Lamb of God! I come, I come!
Be-cause Thy prom-ise I be-lieve; O Lamb of God! I come, I come!

Story of the Cross. Concluded.

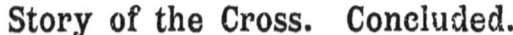

blood did free-ly flow, Till the chil-dren all shall know Of the cross!

No. 89. A Sinner Like Me.

"*Christ Jesus came into the world to save sinners.*" 1 Tim. i: 15.

C. J. B.   C. J. Butler. By per.

1. I was once far a-way from the Sav-iour, And as
2. I wan-dered on in the dark-ness, Not a
3. And then, in that dark, lone-ly hour, . . . A

vile as a sin-ner could be; . . I won-der'd if
ray . . of light could I see; . . And the tho't fill'd my
voice sweetly whis-per'd to me, . . Say-ing, Christ, the Re-

Christ the Re-deem-er, Could save a poor sin-ner like me.
heart with sad-ness, There's no help for a sin-ner like me.
deemer, has pow-er To save a poor sin-ner like me.

4 I listened: and lo! 't was the Saviour
   That was speaking so kindly to me;
   I cried, "I'm the chief of sinners,
   Oh, save a poor sinner like me!"

5 I then fully trusted in Jesus;
   And oh, what a joy came to me!
   My heart was filled with His praises,
   For saving a sinner like me.

6 No longer in darkness I'm walking
   For the light is now shining on me,
   And now unto others I'm telling,
   How He saved a poor sinner like me.

7 And when life's journey is over,
   And I the dear Saviour shall see,
   I'll praise Him for ever and ever.
   For saving a sinner like me.

Copyright, 1881, by John J. Hood.

Sheltered in the Rock of Ages. Concluded.

Safe,
Safe-ly sheltered in the Rock, Safe, so safe, so safe am I.
Safe-ly

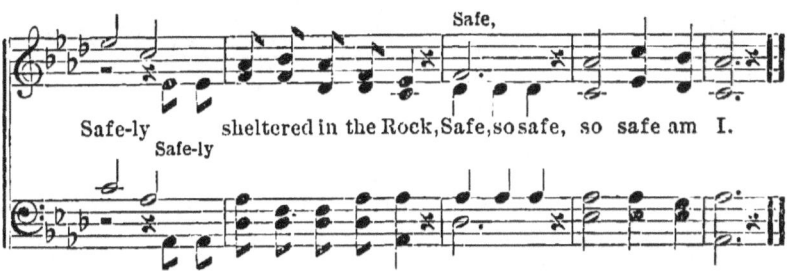

No. 91. There is a Fountain.

William Cowper. Western Melody.

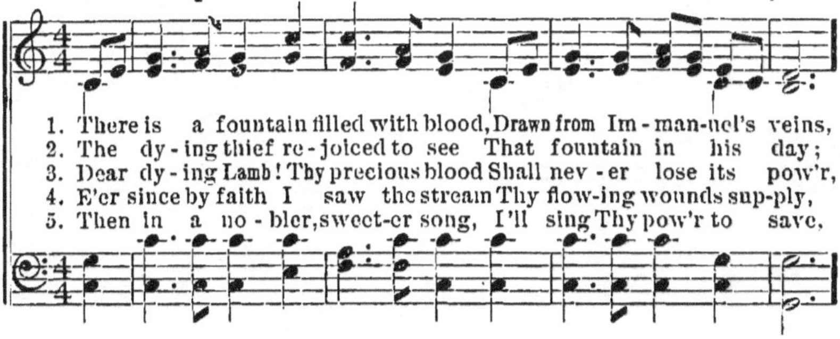
1. There is a fountain filled with blood, Drawn from Im - man-uel's veins,
2. The dy - ing thief re - joiced to see That fountain in his day;
3. Dear dy - ing Lamb! Thy precious blood Shall nev - er lose its pow'r,
4. E'er since by faith I saw the stream Thy flow-ing wounds sup-ply,
5. Then in a no - bler, sweet-er song, I'll sing Thy pow'r to save,

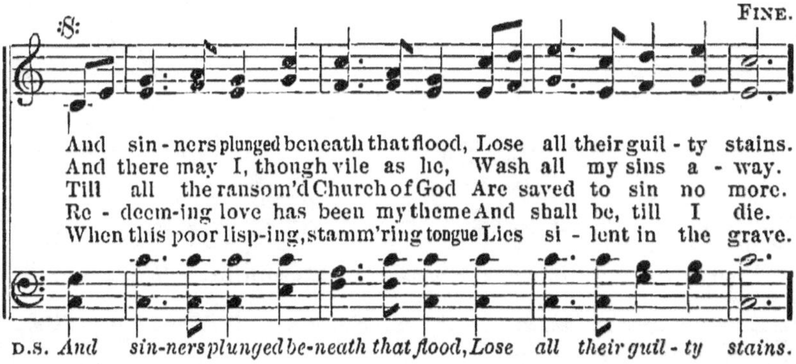
FINE.
And sin - ners plunged beneath that flood, Lose all their guil - ty stains.
And there may I, though vile as he, Wash all my sins a - way.
Till all the ransom'd Church of God Are saved to sin no more.
Re - deem-ing love has been my theme And shall be, till I die.
When this poor lisp-ing, stamm'ring tongue Lies si - lent in the grave.
D.S. And sin-ners plunged be-neath that flood, Lose all their guil - ty stains.

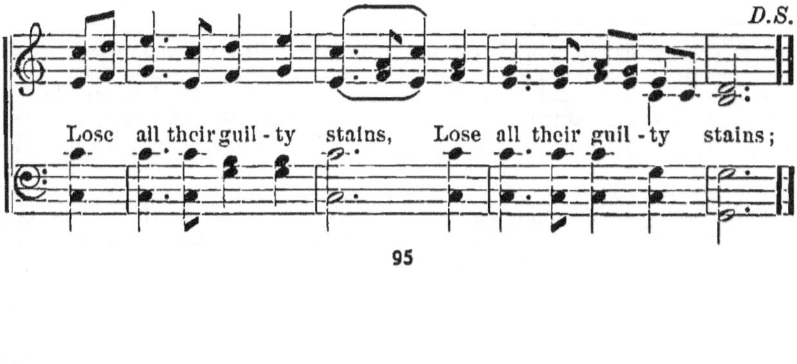
D.S.
Lose all their guil - ty stains, Lose all their guil - ty stains;

No. 92. Fear Not to Trust Me in the Storm.

"It is I; be not afraid." Matt. xiv: 27.

Rev. J. W. Howe.   J. H. Ruebush.

1. Fear not to trust Me in the storm, I'm al-ways ver-y near. I come thy needless fears to calm, Then, weary ones, do n't fear.
2. I may not al-ways seem so near As thou wouldst have Me be; But in the calm and in the storm, I all thy dan-gers see.
3. Fear not to trust My mighty arm; It bro't sal-va-tion down. I suf-fered much to give thee life, To give to thee a crown.

CHORUS.

Fear not, . . I am with thee, Fear not, . . I am with thee, Fear not, . . . I am with thee, . . am with thee all the way.

Fear not, I am with thee, am with thee all way, Fear not, I am with thee, am with thee all way, Fear not, I am with thee, am with thee all way,

4 I'm always near thee in the storm,
   To raise thy sinking feet,
 If only thou wilt trust My word,
   And My commandments keep.

5 Fear not, the storm will soon be o'er,
   The victory soon be won;
 Then lean upon My mighty arm,
   And sing, I'm going home.

6 And when the storm of life is past,
   And you have faithful been,
 I'll take you to that blest abode
   That's not defiled with sin.

7 There no more storms shall cause thee fear;
   The river will be crossed;
 Then thou shalt rest within the gates,
   With all the heavenly host.

Copyright, 1894, by J. H. Ruebush.

No More Good-Byes. Concluded.

No. 95. I Do Believe.
Isaac Watts.

1. A-las! and did my Sav-iour bleed, And did my Sov-'reign die?
2. Was it for crimes that I have done He groaned up-on the tree?
3. But drops of grief can ne'er re-pay The debt of love I owe;

CHO. I do be-lieve, I now be-lieve, That Je-sus died for me;

Would He de-vote that sa-cred head For such a worm as I?
A-maz-ing pit-y, grace un-known, And love be-yond de-gree!
Here, Lord, I give my-self a-way, 'Tis all that I can do.

And thro' His blood, His precious blood, I shall from sin be free.

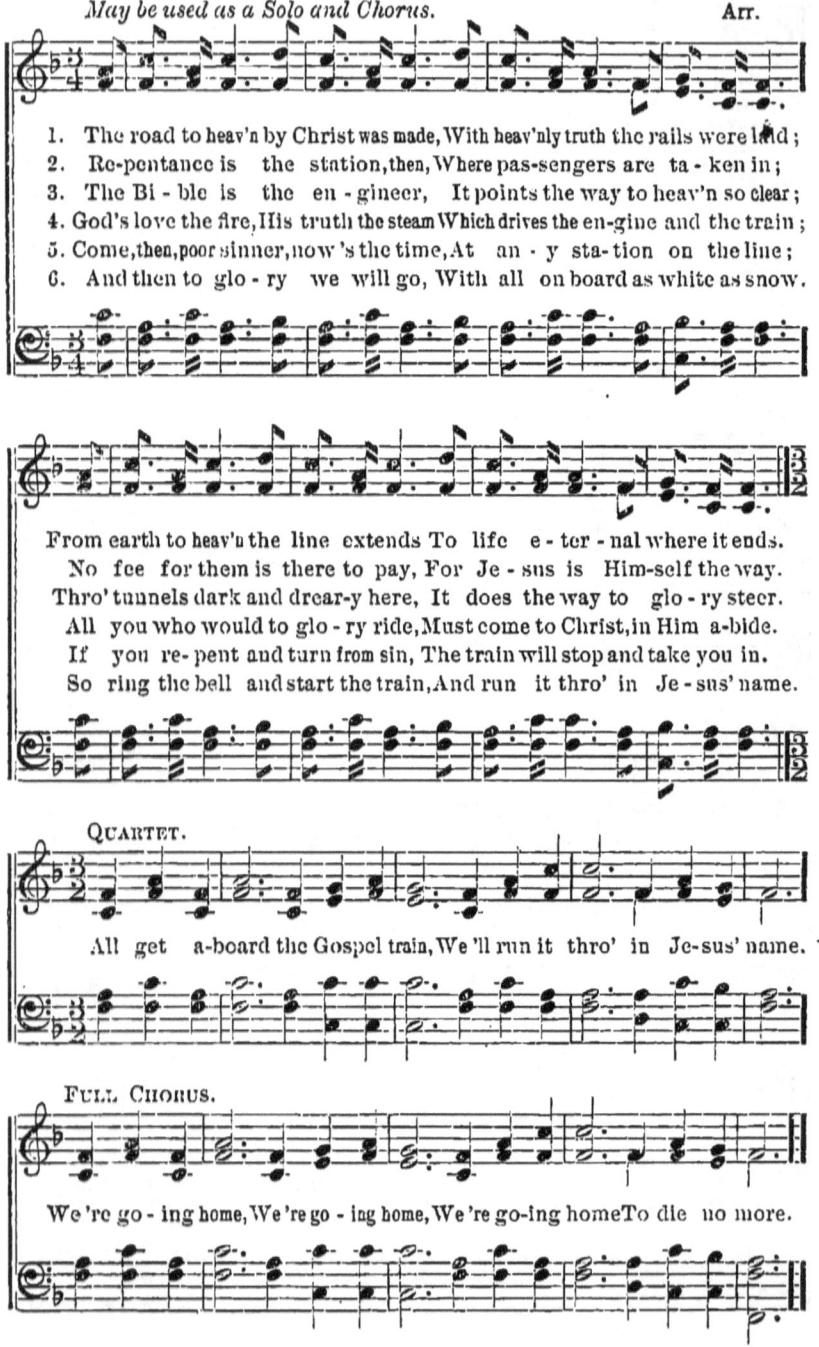

No. 99. **The City of Light.**

A. S. K.   A. S. Kieffer.

1. There's a cit-y of light 'mid the stars, we are told, Where they know not a sor-row or care;
   And the gates are of pearl, and the streets are of gold, And the building ex-ceed-ing-ly fair.
2. Brother dear, nev-er fear,—we shall triumph at last, If we trust in the word He has giv'n;
   When our tri-als and toils, and our weepings are past, We shall meet in that home up in heav'n.

CHORUS.

Let us pray for each oth-er, nor faint by the way, In this sad world of sor-row and care, For that home is so bright, and is al-most in sight, And I trust in my heart you'll go there.

3 Sister dear, never fear,—for the Saviour is near,
  With His hand He will lead you along;
  And the way that is dark Christ will graciously clear,
  And your mourning shall turn to a song.

4 Let us walk in the light of the gospel divine;
  Let us ever keep near to the cross;
  Let us love, watch, and pray, in our pilgrimage here;
  Let us count all things else but as loss.

At the Saviour's Right Hand. Concluded.

No. 101. Thou Thinkest, Lord, of Me.

E. D. Mund. E. S. Lorenz.

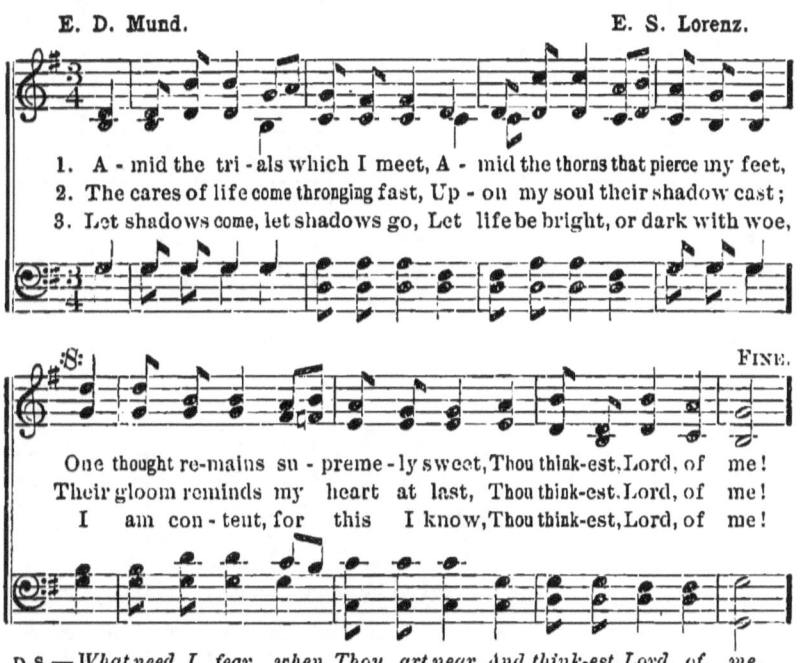

1. A-mid the tri-als which I meet, A-mid the thorns that pierce my feet,
2. The cares of life come thronging fast, Up-on my soul their shadow cast;
3. Let shadows come, let shadows go, Let life be bright, or dark with woe,

One thought remains supremely sweet, Thou think-est, Lord, of me!
Their gloom reminds my heart at last, Thou think-est, Lord, of me!
I am content, for this I know, Thou think-est, Lord, of me!

D.S.—*What need I fear when Thou art near, And think-est, Lord, of me.*

CHORUS.

Thou think-est, Lord, of me, Thou think-est, Lord, of me, of me, of me,

Copyright, 1883, by E. S. Lorenz.

No. 102. What shall it Profit Thee?

M. P. Ferguson.   W. A. Ogden. By per.

1. Oh, what shall it prof-it thee, broth-er, Hous-es and a-cres so broad, No ti-tle to man-sions of glo-ry e-ter-nal, And none to the cit-y of God?
2. Oh, what shall it prof-it thee, broth-er, Friendships to share and to make, And know not the friendships of Je-sus, the Sav-iour, Of Je-sus who died for thy sake?
3. Oh, what shall it prof-it thee, broth-er, Earth-ly am-bi-tion and fame, If Christ in the life-book of glo-ry e-ter-nal, Had nev-er re-cord-ed thy name?

REFRAIN.

What shall it prof-it thee then; . . Tho' the whole world be thine own, . . When the death an-gel has called for thy spir-it, And mer-cy for-ev-er has flown?

Copyright, 1890, by E. O. Excell.

No. 104. The Kingdom Coming.

Mrs. M. B. C. Slade.   R. M. McIntosh. By per.

1. From all the dark pla - ces Of earth's heathen ra - ces, Oh, see how the thick shadows fly! The voice of sal - va - tion A - wakes ev - 'ry na - tion. Come o - ver and help us, they cry.
2. The sun - light is glanc - ing O'er arm - ies ad - vanc - ing To con - quer the king - doms of sin; Our Lord shall pos - sess them, His pres - ence shall bless them, His beau - ty shall en - ter them in.
3. With shout - ing, and sing - ing, And ju - bi - lant ring - ing, Their arms of re - bel - lion cast down, At last ev - 'ry na - tion, The Lord of sal - va - tion, Their King and Re - deem - er shall crown!

CHORUS.

The king - dom is com - ing, Oh, tell ye the sto - ry; God's ban - ner ex - alt - ed shall be! The earth shall be full of His

By per. R. M. McIntosh, owner of copyright.

No. 106. There's a Great Day Coming.

W. L. T.   W. L. Thompson.

1. There's a great day com-ing, A great day coming, There's a great day com-ing by and by, When the saints and the sin-ners shall be part-ed right and left, Are you read-y for that day to come?
2. There's a bright day com-ing, A bright day coming, There's a bright day com-ing by and by, But its bright-ness shall on - ly come to them that love the Lord, Are you read-y for that day to come?
3. There's a sad day com-ing, A sad day coming, There's a sad day com-ing by and by, When the sin - ner shall hear his doom, "De-part I know ye not," Are you read-y for that day to come?

CHORUS.
Are you read-y? Are you read-y? Are you read-y for the Judgment day? Are you ready? Are you ready For the Judgment day?

By permission of W. L. Thompson & Co., East Liverpool, O., and Chicago, Ill.

No. 107. Jesus, Lover of My Soul.

Charles Wesley.   S. B. Marsh.

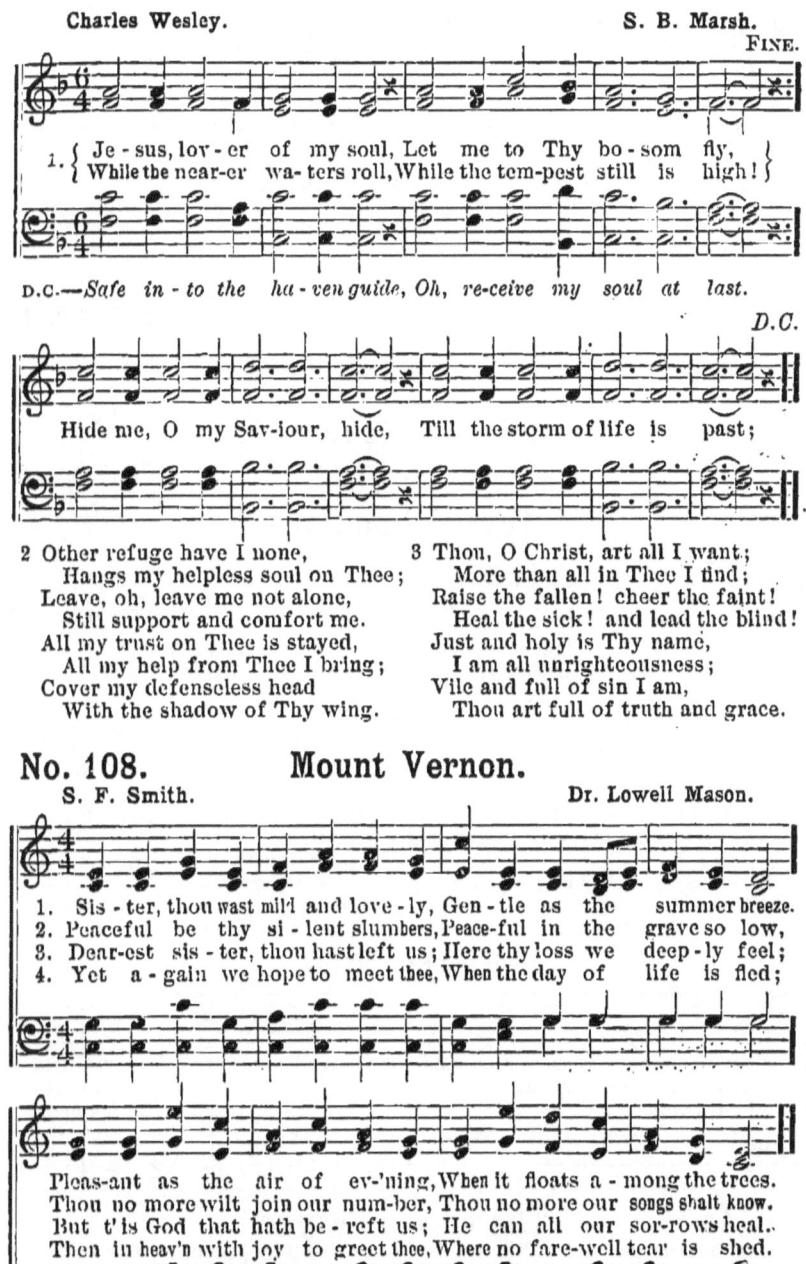

1. { Je-sus, lov-er of my soul, Let me to Thy bo-som fly, }
   { While the near-er wa-ters roll, While the tem-pest still is high! }

D.C.—*Safe in-to the ha-ven guide, Oh, re-ceive my soul at last.*

Hide me, O my Sav-iour, hide, Till the storm of life is past;

2 Other refuge have I none,
  Hangs my helpless soul on Thee;
  Leave, oh, leave me not alone,
  Still support and comfort me.
  All my trust on Thee is stayed,
  All my help from Thee I bring;
  Cover my defenseless head
  With the shadow of Thy wing.

3 Thou, O Christ, art all I want;
  More than all in Thee I find;
  Raise the fallen! cheer the faint!
  Heal the sick! and lead the blind!
  Just and holy is Thy name,
  I am all unrighteousness;
  Vile and full of sin I am,
  Thou art full of truth and grace.

No. 108. Mount Vernon.

S. F. Smith.   Dr. Lowell Mason.

1. Sis-ter, thou wast mild and love-ly, Gen-tle as the summer breeze.
2. Peaceful be thy si-lent slumbers, Peace-ful in the grave so low,
3. Dear-est sis-ter, thou hast left us; Here thy loss we deep-ly feel;
4. Yet a-gain we hope to meet thee, When the day of life is fled;

Pleas-ant as the air of ev-'ning, When it floats a-mong the trees.
Thou no more wilt join our num-ber, Thou no more our songs shalt know.
But t'is God that hath be-reft us; He can all our sor-rows heal.
Then in heav'n with joy to greet thee, Where no fare-well tear is shed.

No. 109. Old Hundred. G. Franc, 1545.

1. Praise God, from whom all blessings flow; Praise Him, all creatures here below;
Praise Him above, ye heav'nly host, Praise Father, Son, and Holy Ghost.

No. 110. "Thy Will be Done."

1. Thy will be done. { In devious way the hurrying stream of } life may run; { Yet still our grateful hearts will say, } Thy will be done.

2 Thy will be | done. || If o'er us shine
A gladdening and a | prosperous |
sun, ||
This prayer will make it more divine, ||
Thy will be | done.

3 Thy will be | done. || Tho' shrouded o'er
Our | path with | gloom, | one comfort, one, |
Is ours to breathe, while we adore, ||
Thy will be | done.

No. 111. Gloria Patri. Anon.

Glory be to the Father, and to the Son, And to the Holy Ghost.
As it was in the beginning, is now, and . . . . ev-er shall be, world without end. A-men.

No. 112. The Lord's Prayer.

Our Father, who art in heaven, hallowed | be Thy | name : || Thy kingdom come, Thy will be done on | earth, as it | is in | heaven;

2 Give us this day our | daily | bread : || and forgive us our trespasses, as we forgive | those who | trespass a- | gainst us.

3 And lead us not into temptation, but de-liver | us from | evil ; || for Thine is the kingdom, and the power, and the glory, for- | ever and | ever. A- | men.

Index.

Title	No.
Arlington	65
A Sinner Like Me	89
At the Beautiful Gate	17
At the Cross I'll Abide	87
At the Saviour's Right Hand	100
Battle Hymn	34
Bear the Torch of the Lord	28
Beulah Land	73
Bring Them In	16
Closer, Lord, to Thee	5
Come to Jesus	67
Come and be Saved	86
Come unto Me	103
Dennis	3
Do They Pray for Me at Home	12
Enough for Me	75
Ever will I Pray	10
Fear Not to Trust Me in the Storm	92
Forever Here my Rest	33
Gates	97
Gloria Patri	111
God's Hand doth Lead Me On	26
God be with You	60
Go and Inquire	61
Hark! the Voice of Jesus Calling	4
Happy Spirits	11
Hiding in the Rock	71
Hosanna	18
How Sweet, How Heavenly	21
Holy Spirit, Faithful Guide	58
I am Washed in the Blood	2
I am Coming to the Cross	13
I am Waiting	68
I am Resting in the Saviour's Love	80
I am with Thee Every Hour	93
I do Believe	95
I Hear Thy Welcome Voice	62
It May be the Last	64
I Long to be There	15
I've been Redeemed	70
I Want to be a Worker	36
I Was a Wandering Sheep	49
Jesus will Welcome Me Home	27
Jesus Died for Me	29
Jesus Calls	30
Jesus, I My Cross Have Taken (No. 1)	32
Jesus, I My Cross Have Taken (No. 2)	35
Jesus Saves	72
Jesus, Lover of My Soul	107
Just as I Am	83
Knocking at the Door	42
Let Me Rest	44
Let Me Cling to Thee	48
Lead Me On	57
Lights Along the Shore	55
Lottie	45
Marching in the Light	20
Mercy for All	82
Mount Vernon	108
My Heart's Prayer	14
Near the Cross	9
Nearer the Cross	51
Nearer, My God, to Thee	77
Nothing but the Blood of Jesus	81
No More Good-byes	94
Old Hundred	109
On Jordan's Stormy Banks	84
Out of Christ	105
Over the Border Land	79
Pray for the Wanderer	23
Praise, Give Praise	40
Revive Us Again	56
Rock of Ages	37
Room at the Cross	69
Safe at Home	39
Sheltered in the Rock of Ages	90
Singing with the Angels	19
Sitting at the Feet of Jesus	25
Sowing Time	59
Story of the Cross	88
Take Up the Cross To-day	8
Tell Us Something More	24
The Cleansing Fountain	7
The Father Calls	22
The Banquet of Love	47
The Child of a King	53
The Heavenly Crown	63
The Unclouded Day	76
The Everlasting Arms	85
The Message of the Angels	96
The Road to Heaven	98
The City of Light	99
The Kingdom Coming	104
The Lord's Prayer	112
There is a Fountain	91
There's a Great Day Coming	106
Thou Thinkest, Lord, of Me	101
Thy Will be Done	110
Title Clear	38
Toiling for Jesus	52
Under His Wings	43
Was it for Me	31
Wandering Home	50
We'll Work till Jesus Comes	41
What a Friend We Have in Jesus	6
What Shall Our Record Be	74
What Shall it Profit Thee	102
What a Glorious Redeemer	78
When the Shining Gates Unfold	66
Why Stand Ye Here Idle	1
Wonderful Grace	1

F. H. GILSON COMPANY, MUSIC TYPOGRAPHERS, BOSTON, MASS.

www.ingramcontent.com/pod-product-compliance
Lightning Source LLC
Chambersburg PA
CBHW020138170426
43199CB00010B/789